# TRUTH
# *CONSEQUENCES*

## Catherine Athans, Ph.D.

ANGELS ISLAND PRESS
Los Altos, CA

Angels Island Press
An Angels Island Production
303 First Street
Los Altos, CA 94022
www.AngelsIsland.com
1-888-58ANGEL

ISBN 978-0-9794380-5-9

Printed in the United States of America

Design: Dotti Albertine, www.AlbertineBookDesign.com
Images: Getty/Thinkstock Images

*To all truth seekers*

*throughout the world*

*who hold the light for everyone.*

*The truth you seek is already inside you.*

*Just remove the lies and it will appear.*

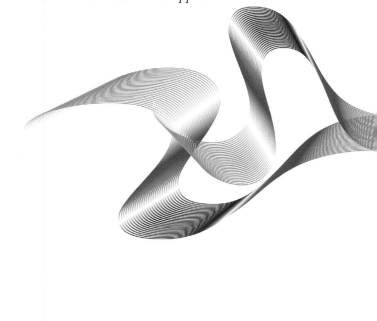

# How do you begin to know truth?

START BY GIVING attention to your inner self. Allow yourself to believe what you uncover. You are taught to believe others and to discount yourself.

**Your truth feels good, feels happy.** Your truth is peaceful and refreshing.

You already have the ability to know truth by going into your heart.

Learning the truth of who you are will give you the knowledge and ability to have a wonderful life.

The truth you seek is already inside you. **Just remove what is hiding your knowing.**

You begin to know truth when you are willing to practice discernment where you will pay attention and consider the places within yourself that show you who you are and where you are going.

**You begin to know truth when you are willing to take action on your intuitive feeling of peace.**

You begin to know truth when you **validate that intuitive feeling** and allow more of the same.

You begin to know truth when you have a new understanding of **what is really necessary** in your life and what is not.

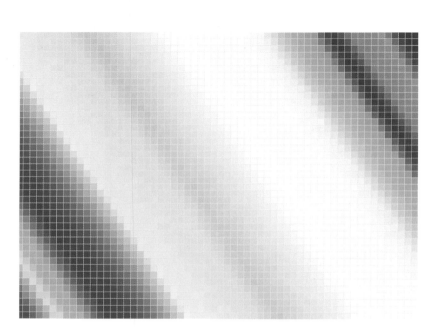

You begin to know truth when you allow yourself to **discern** as part of your daily routine.

**Truth grows
with attention
and love**

Catherine Athans, Ph.D.

You begin to know truth when you allow yourself the courage to go inside and let go of lie.

You begin to know truth when you allow your capability to know choices, possibilities and answers.

Truth grows with attention and love.

Truth grows with you as the active participant and with you as the active observer.

**Using your intuition and discernment you have great tools to see through lie.**

You can know that any seemingly negative event can inspire and propel you to what is true.

With truth you have plenty of air to breathe below the surface.

You can discover that decisions are multifaceted, brilliant energies that you can blend with truth to open to a larger you.

**With truth you can use your imagination to increase love.**

With truth you feel a lovely sense of anticipation and enthusiasm for your adventures through life and what new and exciting understandings you will gain.

**With truth your heart automatically opens to you, giving you more insight and information regarding your best path to follow.**

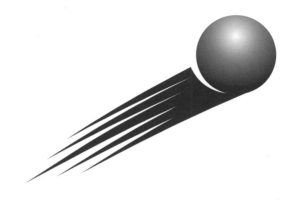

14    Catherine Athans, Ph.D.

# What is Meant by Giving Your Inner Truth Energy?

THIS MEANS THAT you make valid what you discern to be truthful for you. You validate your inner knowing instead of what others—society or the outside world—have decided should be your truth.

**Stop a moment here. Think about the last time someone asked you for your inner truth.**

Can you recall the last time you went inside yourself and asked yourself for the whole, unadulterated truth?

When you practice discernment, you will pay attention to, and consider the places within yourself, that show you the way and provide you with the truth of who you are and where you are going.

As you allow your skill of discernment to be active and pursue the truth of who you are really are, your entire energy system will be activated with truth. This dissolves all ideas, programs and senses that are not yours—that belong to a lie.

**By dissolving lie you emerge as a being of more light, with more energy and enthusiasm.** You go forward in your life manifesting what truly are your heart's desires.

You begin to know yourself from a very different, deep level. As you allow this knowledge to pour forth through you, new experiences and opportunities open. You as a being of light function through your consciousness of your own truth. **You are built on truth.**

**The truth is that**

**you are meant to have self-love,**

**self-esteem and self-regard.**

**You are meant to be a magnificent,**

**brilliant human being...**

**at one with nature, with one another,**

**full of love, life and truth ...**

**regardless of your religious beliefs,**

**your race, your gender,**

**your socio-economic status.**

**As you go forward in truth**

**the universe will open to you**

**avenues that were previously not seen**

**and were deemed to be impossible.**

# Truth vs. Lie

1. **Truth fills and lie empties.**
   When you allow yourself to be with truth, you begin to feel full, whole, peaceful and free.

2. **Truth loves and lie fears.**
   When you are told the truth and when you speak truth, you feel the love.

3. **Truth nourishes. Lie sickens.**
   You begin to know truth when you look outside and see a beautiful flower. You simply feel good looking at the flower. That's truth.

4. **Truth is friendly. Lie is your enemy.**

   You begin to know truth when you turn the corner and someone notices you, smiles and says, "good day." That lovely feeling you have is truth.

5. **Truth guides. Lie misleads.**

   You begin to know truth when you are willing to go inside and listen to your heart.

6. **Truth is more than intuition.**

   You begin to know truth when you are willing to take action on your intuitive feelings.

7. **Truth sees clearly.**

   You can look at any seemingly negative event and see the truth that can inspire and propel you to be greater.

## 8. Truth is peaceful.

When you tell yourself the truth you create peace of mind.

## 9. Truth feels good.

With truth your heart automatically opens, giving you more insight, information and joy.

## 10. Truth is happy.

With truth you feel a lovely sense of anticipation and enthusiasm for your adventures throughout your whole life.

## 11. Truth is refreshing.

When you are willing to hear, feel and see truth every cell in your body is energized with new life.

### 12. Truth creates health.

Speaking the truth activates all of your immune systems, restoring your natural health.

### 13. Truth opens your path.

When you allow truth to lead you the blocks that you thought were there disappear.

### 14. Truth develops courage.

You begin to know truth when you allow yourself to go inside and let go of the lie.

Lie feels heavy.

Lie feels dirty.

Lie feels bad.

Lie feels angry.

Lie feels vindictive.

Lie creates illness.

Lie is blind.

The truth stands by itself. Lie needs to deceive.

**Whenever you encounter the negative and fill it with love, it transmutes into truth.**

# What Can You Expect?

DEVELOPING YOUR SKILL of knowing truth will teach you to know which possibilities and choices resonate as harmonious and true for you. **When you practice knowing truth, you begin to open and discover new parts of yourself.** This discovery, this unveiling, will lead you to a new understanding of self, including what you value and who you are when you are being true to yourself. As you continue this inner journey, you discover more and more facets of truth. You become that amazing kaleidoscope of infinite colors, textures, and dimensions.

# How Do You Know Who You Are?

*How have you learned who you are?*
*What is it like for you to go inside?*
*How do you know yourself from others?*
*How do you know when you have accepted lie?*

THIS HAPPENS IN a very subtle manner. When energy is foreign, yet elusive—your system and your being may incorporate it without your conscious knowledge. **You may have been taking on another's energy because of your sympathy for them or from early programming of lie regarding who you are.**

When you take on this foreign lie-energy, it throws your system out of balance, and the system remains out of balance until a crisis of truth is able to break through.

This crisis of truth often is interpreted as something bad. But indeed it is a blessing, because it allows more room for you to exist in your life, in your mind, and in your body. **It allows for you to live a vibrant life in truth that lets go of all that is not you, that lets go of all of you that has been a lie.**

# You Are Unique.

WHAT MAKES YOU uniquely you?

Once you begin to allow yourself to feel truth, your perception of who and what you are changes.

**As you come to know truth from lie, the activity of knowing more truth becomes like a fun game of adventure.** It allows you to examine how you perceive life's choices and how you allow or disallow truth to be active in you.

Getting to know your self by going within starts the interesting voyage of discovering truth.

You will find an abundance of feelings and previously hidden understandings as you go deeper.

**Allow yourself to become reacquainted with yourself through your quest to discover truth.**

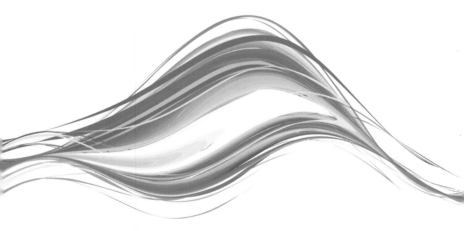

# The Role of Imagination

WHEN SEEKING TRUTH, please remember to allow your imagination to be very large, in full color and in full movement.

**Imagination is the act or power of forming mental images of what may not be actually present or what may not have actually been experienced.**

Imagination is more than a faculty of the mind. Imagination is a flowing, intuitive gift. It is the ability to see what could be.

Imagination is bringing into being—from little or nothing—great riches.

Imagination is the first tool that you need to manifest, to create your truth.

The process of imagining provides you with an avenue to have greater participation in your own life, for it is your imagination, your thoughts, which create your perceptions of the world in which you live.

**Think of this? You are the one perceiving your world.**

Because of this you are the one who may change your perception. Imagination is a key in doing this. Taking the time to activate your imagination is key to obtaining what is true for you in your life.

**Please take a moment and consider the following. Nothing exists today that wasn't first imagined.**

# The Role of Intuition

EINSTEIN SAID INTUITION IS GREATER THAN KNOWLEDGE.

Intuition is defined as the direct perception of truth.

**The person who lives life through INTUITION lives in a state of truth and in a state of grace**.

Intuition allows one to defy the three-dimensional laws and allows things to manifest that may appear to be seemingly impossible.

Using your intuition is key in knowing truth and creating a sense of joy.

**Another key to amplifying truth is to allow your intuition to have free reign.** So often intuition is ignored for something that we deem more reasonable. We tend to honor logic and demean intuition.

However, life does not operate logically.

**Logic often leads one down a path of lie.**

As you become more familiar with how your intuition feels inside, you begin to use it more.

As you begin to allow yourself to feel what truth feels like, pay attention to your whole body and see and feel the changes it is making as you do this.

**Intuition can be a thought or feeling that literally comes to you out of the BLUE.**

The **BLUE** is the great sea of source from which all things come. It can also be part of your inner guidance that you call upon when making decisions.

Have you ever wanted to find out some piece of information and you turn the corner, look up at the sign, and get your answer?

**Out of the BLUE is literally out of the vast, infinite source of life.** It is responding to your sincere, truthful desire to Know.

Do you ever have a sense about something that really can't be explained? That is your intuition.

**Do you ever have a gut feeling about something? That is your intuition.**

It is vital to allow your intuition to be active and available in your life.

It is the foundation that allows you to experience, see, feel, and know truth.

**Give yourself permission to be with your intuition. Allow yourself to know truth.**

Please take a moment now to give yourself permission to be with truth.

# How does it feel
# to allow truth into your life?

# The Role of Discernment

DISCERNMENT IS A powerful tool to assist you in knowing what is true for you.

**To discern is to perceive or recognize one thing from another—to develop your insight, your knowledge, your intuition** and your recognition of the differences and shades of differences in the choices that are presented to you daily.

To discern is to separate truth from untruth.

Using discernment you are able to search and know the fine nuances and differences between that which is the precious truth and that which is the lie that deceives.

Actively using your imagination and your skill of discernment, you receive the truth of your heart's desires, and you are able to manifest the truth in all your mind, body and affairs.

**Every cell in your body communicates with every other cell.**

**Every cell in your body**

**tells the truth.**

# The Body Knows

TO DEVELOP A relationship with the body is one of the most important things you can do to be healthy.

**Your body is made of truth. Your body will always tell you the truth if you are willing to listen.**

This is the issue. You have to stop, look and learn to listen to your heart, your gut and your whole self.

*What feelings do you have in your body that let you know that something is true for you?*

*What feelings do you have in your body that let you know that something is not true?*

Pay attention to the differences of these feelings.

# GO INTO YOUR HEART.

As you go into your heart and learn what is the truth for you and what this feels like, you begin to understand yourself from a divine place.

You begin to have a more divine perspective of love, joy, and happiness.

As you free yourself from the lies that have been dictated to you, and for you, and know the truth, you begin to connect with your core essence. **You learn what it is that will lead you to true joy and happiness.**

You will learn what lies have been creating disharmony and dis-ease within you. You gain new courage and new resolve and start on a new path of truth in your life. As you pursue this path of truth, each success breeds more success.

**Each truth breeds more truth and you begin to have a greater understanding of yourself, of the universe, and your place in the universe.** It is in every one of us to be wise, to know what it is that we are truly here to accomplish.

Pursuing the truth with discernment and acting with intuition and insight lead to a fuller, richer, happier life.

As the impossible becomes not just the possible, but rather the daily occurrence, you come to expect and receive the impossible truths and you are always delighted with how much wonder there is in each moment of your day.

Please become a more positive participant in your life through making wise choices. **Please acknowledge that you already have the ability to discern and know those truths which are right for you.** It is up to you to utilize and exercise these skills of discernment, intuition and truth when making life decisions.

Tools to assist you in developing the skill of discernment include:

*Thought*
*Journaling*
*Discerning*
*Meditating*
*Affirmations*
*Practice*

Joy is waiting for you!

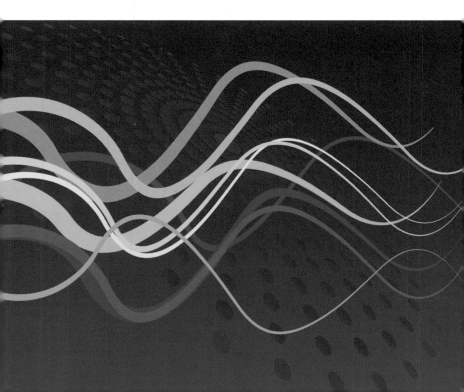

## Exercise to know truth

BREATHE, GO INSIDE, and ask the following questions of your heart, your gut and your total being.

*What do I feel?*
*Heart, what do you feel?*
*Gut, what do you feel?*

Pay attention and allow whatever is felt to be valid.

*Where do I feel calm?*
*Where do I feel upset?*

Breathe into the calm and breathe out from the calm.

*How do you feel?*

Now take the calm and breathe calm into the upset and breathe the calm out from the upset.

*How do you feel?*

You may wish to repeat breathing the calm into the upset and breathing the calm out from the upset.

Ask yourself,
*Am I now feeling peaceful?*

**Practice takes time.** Give yourself the time each day to practice. 10 minutes in the morning and 10 minutes in the evening.

Pay attention and jot down in your journal feelings of joy and feelings of peace. **Give yourself a month and notice how much more truth has been established in your life.**

*Pay attention to your thoughts.*
*Pay attention to your choices.*

Do you have a feeling of peace?
Or do you have feelings of anxiety or frustration?
This is the time to stop and ask yourself, **"Are these my feelings? Are these feelings truth or lie?"** … remembering the qualities of truth and letting go the feelings of lie.

**Go on an adventure of the self.** Explore your innocence. Participate and contribute more to the truth you find. Please know that your inner self is safe.

Give yourself validity for what comes from within you, and allow it to come forward without judgment. Let your innocence, your freedom from judgment of others, your freedom from judgment of self, be present, heard and activated in your life.

Innocence places you in a state of grace, where only miracles can happen. **A state of grace is that state where there is only truth and love.** When you come back and are willing to allow innocence to be active in your life you come back to the source and are able to allow more truth in your life. Innocence brings a state of bliss.

Ask yourself often, "Is this belief that I carry Truth or Lie?" How do you know? Is the belief heavy? Does it feel good or bad? Does it come with ease? Does it create ease in your life? Is it a block? Is it a weight. Does it stop you as you are opening your heart to your dreams?

**Truth is light, airy,
and facilitating.
Lie blocks.**

**Look deeper.
Allow yourself to know truth.
Breathe truth into your belly.
Now allow truth to
breathe into your entire body.**

Pause and let go.